© 2003 by Barbour Publishing, Inc.

ISBN 1-59310-409-X

Unless otherwise noted, Scripture quotations are taken from the King James Version of the Bible.

Scripture quotations marked NIV are taken from the HOLY BIBLE, NEW INTERNATIONAL VERSION®. NIV®. Copyright © 1973, 1978, 1984 by International Bible Society. Used by permission of Zondervan Publishing House. All rights reserved.

Definitions are taken from *Merriam-Webster's Collegiate Dictionary.*

Cover image © Pictures Now

Published by Barbour Publishing, Inc., P.O. Box 719, Uhrichsville, Ohio 44683, www.barbourbooks.com

Our mission is to publish and distribute inspirational products offering exceptional value and biblical encouragement to the masses.

Member of the
Evangelical Christian
Publishers Association

Printed in China.
5 4 3 2 1

Wishing You a Merry Christmas

KELLY WILLIAMS

W e

wish you a

merry christmas;

WE WISH YOU
A MERRY
CHRISTMAS; We wish

you a merry christmas and a Happy New Year. Good tidings we bring to you

and your kin; Good tidings for Christmas and

a Happy New Year. We wish you a merry

christmas; We wish you a merry christmas; We

wish you a merry christmas and a Happy New

Year. Good tidings we bring to you and your kin;

Good tidings for Christmas

a n d a H a p p y

N e w Y e a r .

Traditional Carol

This Christmas I wish you. . .

Hope

Hope

n. desire accompanied by

expectation of or belief in

fulfillment.

And she shall bring forth a son,

and thou shalt call his name JESUS:

for he shall save his people from their sins.

MATTHEW 1:21

Time was with most of us, when Christmas Day, encircling all our limited world like a magic ring, left nothing out for us to miss or seek; bound together all our home enjoyments, affections, and hopes; grouped everything and everyone round the Christmas fire, and made the little picture shining in our bright young eyes, complete.

CHARLES DICKENS

Dear Lord,

Help me to keep my eyes fixed on You

throughout the Christmas season.

When the commercialism of the holiday threatens to

snuff out the real meaning of Christmas in my heart,

remind me of the gift of Hope

You sent on that silent night so long ago.

Amen.

O
little
town of
Bethlehem,
HOW STILL we see thee lie!
Above thy deep and dreamless sleep
the silent stars go by.
Yet in thy dark streets shineth
the everlasting Light;
The hopes and fears of all the years
are met in thee
TO - night.

Phillips Brooks

*May you have hope in your heart
each day of the year!*

THIS IS CHRISTMAS: NOT THE TINSEL, NOT THE GIVING
AND RECEIVING, NOT EVEN THE CAROLS, BUT THE
HUMBLE HEART THAT RECEIVES ANEW THE WONDROUS
GIFT, THE CHRIST.

FRANK MCKIBBEN

Now when Jesus was born in Bethlehem of Judaea in
the days of Herod the king, behold, there came wise
men from the east to Jerusalem, saying, Where is he that
is born King of the Jews? for we have seen his star in
the east, and are come to worship him.

MATTHEW 2:1–2

I am not alone at all, I thought. *I was never alone at all.* And that, of course, is the message of Christmas. We are never alone. Not when the night is darkest, the wind coldest, the world seemingly most indifferent. For this is still the time God chooses.

TAYLOR CALDWELL

O come, O come, Emmanuel,
And ransom captive Israel,
That mourns in lonely exile here
Until the Son of God appear.
Rejoice! Rejoice!
Emmanuel shall come to thee, O Israel.

LATIN HYMN

This Christmas I wish you. . .

Joy

Joy

n. a source or

cause of delight

Joy to the world, the Lord is come!
Let earth receive her King;
Let every heart prepare Him room,
And heaven and nature sing,
And heaven and nature sing,
And heaven, and heaven, and nature sing.

ISAAC WATTS

From home to home and heart to heart,
from one place to another.
The warmth and joy of Christmas
brings us closer to each other.

Emily Matthews

May you find joy—
not only at Christmastime—
but in the everyday
miracles of life.

Angels

we have

heard on

high

Sweetly singing o'er the
plains, And the mountains
in reply Echoing their JOYOUS
s t r a i n s .
Gloria, in excelsis Deo!
Gloria, in excelsis Deo!
Shepherds, why this jubilee? Why your joyous strains prolong? What the
gladsome tidings be Which inspire your heavenly song?
Gloria, in excelsis Deo!
Gloria, in excelsis Deo!

Come to Bethlehem and see
Christ whose birth the angels
sing; Come, adore on bended knee, Christ the Lord, the
newborn King.

Traditional French Carol

Lord Jesus,

*Please forgive me for being grumpy as
I trudge through the never-ending tasks
set before me this holiday season.
My to-do list seems to keep growing with
shopping, church services, and family gatherings—
and I'm running short on time!
Restore the joy of Christmas to my heart. . .
and help me to relax each day and make time for*

You—

my one true Source of Joy.

Somehow, not only for Christmas,

But all the long year through,

The joy that you give to others,

Is the joy that comes back to you.

John Greenleaf Whittier

When they saw the star,

they were overjoyed. . . .

They saw the child with his mother Mary,

and they bowed down and worshiped him.

Then they opened their treasures

and presented him with gifts.

MATTHEW 2:10–11 NIV

As with gladness, men of old
Did the guiding star behold
As with joy they hailed its light
Leading onward, beaming bright
So, most glorious Lord, may we
Evermore be led to Thee.

WILLIAM C. DIX

This Christmas I wish you...

Peace

Peace

n. freedom from

disquieting or oppressive

thoughts or emotions

For unto us a child is born,
unto us a son is given:
and the government shall be
upon his shoulder:
and his name shall be called
Wonderful, Counsellor,
The mighty God,
The everlasting Father,
The Prince of Peace.

ISAIAH 9:6

*Advent is the perfect time to clear and prepare the Way.
Advent is a winter training camp for those who desire peace.
By reflection and prayer, by reading and meditation, we
can make our hearts a place where a blessing of peace would
desire to abide and where the birth of the Prince of Peace
might take place.*

EDWARD HAYS

WE HAVE PEACE
WITH GOD THROUGH
OUR LORD JESUS CHRIST.

ROMANS 5:1 NIV

Peace, like charity,
begins at home.

FRANKLIN D. ROOSEVELT

What is Christmas? . . .

It is a fervent wish that every cup

may overflow with blessings rich and eternal,

and that every path may lead to peace.

AGNES M. PHARO

Dear Heavenly Father,

Please offer peace to the hearts of families
as they struggle through the hustle and bustle
of the holiday season.
We are in such a rush to
accomplish our everyday tasks—
and now with the Christmas holiday in our midst,
the days are much more hectic.
Remind us all of the importance of family
and of the awesome meaning of Christmas—
as You sent the gift of Your Son.
Help us to slow down and to take a moment
to reflect on Your love daily.
Amen.

I heard the bells on Christmas Day
Their old familiar carols play,
And wild and sweet the words repeat
Of peace on Earth, good will to men!

HENRY WADSWORTH LONGFELLOW

*Seek the presence of God...
and in His arms
you will find peace.*

And suddenly there was with the angel a multitude of the heavenly host praising God, and saying, Glory to God in the highest, and on earth peace, good will toward men. And it came to pass, as the angels were gone away from them into heaven, the shepherds said one to another, Let us now go even unto Bethlehem, and see this thing which is come to pass, which the Lord hath made known unto us.

LUKE 2:13–15

For he himself is our peace.

EPHESIANS 2:14 NIV

Silent

Night, holy

N i g h t ,

All is calm,

all is bright Round

yon virgin mother and Child. Holy Infant,

so tender and mild, Sleep in heavenly peace,

SLEEP   in   HEAVENLY

P E A C E .

Silent Night, holy Night, All is calm, all

is bright Round yon virgin

mother and Child. HOLY INFANT, SO

TENDER AND MILD, Sleep in heavenly

peace, Sleep in   h e a v e n l y

p e a c e .

Josef Mohr

This Christmas I wish you...

Love

 *Love*

n. unselfish loyal and

benevolent concern for

the good of another

LOVE is patient, love is kind.
It does not envy, it does not boast,
it is not proud. It is not rude,
it is not self-seeking,
it is not easily angered,
it keeps no record of wrongs.
Love does not delight in evil
but rejoices with the truth.
It always protects, always trusts,
always hopes, always perseveres.
1 CORINTHIANS 13:4–7 NIV

CHRISTMAS—
that magic blanket that wraps itself about us,
that something so intangible that it is like a fragrance.
It may weave a spell of nostalgia.
Christmas may be a day of feasting, or of prayer,
but always it will be a day of remembrance—
a day in which we think of everything we have ever loved.

AUGUSTA E. RUNDEL

LOVE CAME DOWN AT CHRISTMAS,
LOVE ALL LOVELY, LOVE DIVINE;
LOVE WAS BORN AT CHRISTMAS;
STAR AND ANGELS GAVE THE SIGN.

CHRISTINA ROSSETTI

Are you willing to believe that love is the strongest thing in the world—
stronger than hate, stronger than evil, stronger than death—
and that the blessed life which began in Bethlehem nineteen hundred
years ago is the image and brightness of the Eternal Love?
Then you can keep Christmas.

HENRY VAN DYKE

Best of all, Christmas means a spirit of love, a time when the love of
God and the love of our fellow men should prevail over all hatred and
bitterness, a time when our thoughts and deeds and the spirit of our lives
manifest the presence of God.

GEORGE F. MCDOUGALL

BLESSED IS
THE SEASON WHICH ENGAGES
THE WHOLE WORLD IN
A CONSPIRACY OF LOVE.

HAMILTON WRIGHT MABI

Let us remember that the Christmas heart is a giving heart, a wide open heart that thinks of others first. The birth of the baby Jesus stands as the most significant event in all history, because it has meant the pouring into a sick world of the healing medicine of love which has transformed all manner of hearts for almost two thousand years. . . . Underneath all the bulging bundles is this beating Christmas heart.

GEORGE MATTHEW ADAMS

CHRISTMAS. . .is not an eternal event at all, but a piece of one's home that one carries in one's heart.

FREYA STARK

The joy of brightening other lives,
bearing each others' burdens,
easing others' loads and
supplanting empty hearts and lives with generous gifts
becomes for us the magic of Christmas.

W. C. JONES

Thank you, Lord,

for the gift of Your love.

May I be a shining

example of that love to others.

Amen.

HOLD GOD'S LOVE
IN YOUR HEART. . .
AND SPREAD HIS LOVE
TO OTHERS
THIS HOLIDAY SEASON—
AND ALWAYS.

*May you have the gladness of
Christmas which is Hope;
The spirit of Christmas
which is Peace;
The heart of Christmas
which is Love.*

AVA V. HENDRICKS